My Country
France

Annabelle Lynch

W
FRANKLIN WATTS

This edition 2013

First published in 2012
by Franklin Watts

Copyright © Franklin Watts 2012

Franklin Watts
338 Euston Road
London NW1 3BH

Franklin Watts Australia
Level 17/207 Kent Street
Sydney, NSW 2000

All rights reserved.

Dewey number: 944'.08412
ISBN: 978 1 4451 2698 2

Printed in Malaysia

Series Editor: Paul Rockett
Series Designer: Paul Cherrill for
  Basement68
Picture Researcher: Diana Morris

Franklin Watts is a division of
Hachette Children's Books,
an Hachette UK company.

www.hachette.co.uk

Every attempt has been made to clear copyright. Should there
be any inadvertent omission please apply to the publisher for
rectification.

Picture credits: auremar/Shutterstock: 13t; Marta Benavides/
istockphoto: front cover cl; Kevin Calvin/Alamy: 12; Alexander
Chaikin/Shutterstock: 7t; Tor Eigeland/Alamy: front cover c, 4,
13b, 16b, 22; Fretschi/Shutterstock: 20b; Robert Fried/Alamy:
15; Botond Horvath/Shutterstock: 9; Pierre Jacques/Hemis/
Alamy: 11; JeniFoto/Shutterstock: 5; Robert Linton/istockphoto:
13c; Maugli/Shutterstock: 1, 21; Phillip Minnis /Shutterstock: 20t;
mountainpix /Shutterstock: 3, 17t; Luba V Nel/Shutterstock:
19; PHB.cz Richard Semik/Shutterstock: 7b; Photononstop/
Superstock: 10; Radius/Superstock: 14; Ray Roberts/Alamy:
16c; Samot/Shutterstock: 2, 8; Paul Tavener/Alamy: 18; Paul
Villecourt/Watts: 6; witchcraft/Shutterstock: front cover cr;
Stephan Zabel/istockphoto: 17b.

Contents

All words in **bold**
appear in the
glossary on page 23.

France in the world

> *Bonjour!* My name is Camille and I come from France.

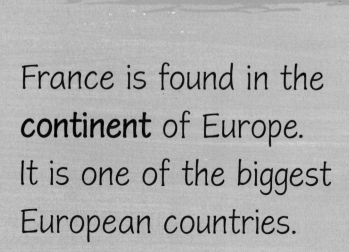

Paris •

Strasbourg •

Marseille •

France's place in the world

France is found in the **continent** of Europe. It is one of the biggest European countries.

strasbourg has many old buildings.

I live in the city of Strasbourg. Strasbourg is the **capital** of a region called Alsace.

People who live in France

Over 65 million people live in France today. Over the years, people from all over the world have come to live here.

My classmates have family from Italy, Asia and Africa.

Most people in France live in or near big cities, such as Paris and Marseille, where there are lots of jobs. Fewer people live in the countryside.

This is Paris, the capital city of France.

My aunt and cousin live in the countryside, and have a pet donkey!

What France looks like

France's **landscape** changes from place to place. There are big cities, but there are also green forests and high mountains.

Around France there are lots of **vineyards** where grapes are grown.

In the east of France, you can find snowy mountains. Along the south and west **coasts** there are long, sandy beaches where people go to swim, surf and have fun!

This is Biarritz, where we go surfing on our holidays.

At home with my family

If the weather is good we eat outside.

Family life is important in France. Most families eat together every evening and at weekends. Meals can go on for a long time.

At weekends and on special days, we often get together with grandparents, aunts, uncles and cousins.

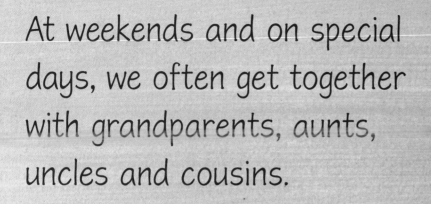

What we eat

French people love good food! France makes some of the best cheese, bread and wine in the world.

We eat long loaves of bread called baguettes with most meals.

Favourite French snacks include croissants or crêpes (pancakes). For a main meal, we often eat cassoulet which is a type of **stew** with beans, sausage and duck.

What would you put on this crêpe?

We eat bread with cassoulet to mop up all the sauce.

I eat croissants for breakfast. What do you have?

Going to school

In France, we start school at six years old at an *école primaire*. I go to an *école primaire*. When you are 11, you move on to a *collège*. From 15 to 18, you go to a different school called a *lycée*.

My brother on the steps of his new school.

14

We have a long lunch every day, and lots of people go home to eat. At many schools, every Wednesday afternoon, we have free time to play sport or enjoy music.

Football is the most popular sport in France.

Having fun

When we're not at school or work, we have fun! Lots of people spend time outside playing. At home, we watch TV and play games such as table tennis.

A lot of people enjoy cycling around France.

I love going to the pool with my friends in the summer. What do you like doing?

During the summer holidays, lots of French people go camping or head to the beach. In winter, they go to the mountains where they can ski, skate or **snowboard**.

The French Alps are a great place to go snowboarding.

We go camping every year. It's fun!

Festivals and celebrations

There are **festivals** throughout the year in France. On 14 July, we celebrate Bastille Day to remember the beginning of the French Revolution in 1789.

On Bastille Day there are lots of parties and fireworks.

Around France, there are smaller festivals. These often celebrate things that are special to a place, such as **local** foods, or remember something that happened there.

In Menton, in the south of France, they have a festival to celebrate the growing of lemons.

Things to see

France has wonderful places to visit! In Paris, you can climb the famous Eiffel Tower and look out all over the city. You can also enjoy a boat ride on the river Seine.

The Eiffel Tower is one of the most recognisable buildings in the world!

Travelling on the river Seine is a great way to see Paris.

In the countryside, there are many famous castles where you can find out all about the past. There are also beautiful parks, mountains and beaches to see.

This is Chenonceau Castle. It was built in 1513.

Here are some facts about my country!

Fast facts about France

Capital city = Paris

Population = 65,350,000

Area = 547,030km2

Language = French

National holiday = 14 July (Bastille Day)

Currency = the Euro

Main religions = Roman Catholic, Muslim, Protestant, Jewish

Longest river = the Loire (1,012km)

Highest mountain = Mont Blanc (4,810m)

Glossary

capital the most important city in a country

coast where the land meets the sea

continent one of the seven main areas of land in the world

festival a special time when people celebrate something

French Revolution when the people of France came together
  in 1789 to change how the country was run

landscape what a place or area looks like

local belonging to a particular place

snowboard to slide down a snowy slope on a special board

stew a meal, usually of meat and vegetables, that is cooked slowly

vineyard an area where grapes are grown to make wine

Websites

www.bbc.co.uk/schools/primaryfrench/
A useful site that helps you learn simple French words.

www.channel4learning.com/sites/wearefrom/france/introduction.html
A good general guide to France, with videos and quirky facts.

http://paris.arounder.com/
Take a virtual tour of Paris and its main landmarks.

Books

My Holiday in France by Susie Brooks (Wayland, 2010)

Been There: France by Annabel Savery (Franklin Watts, 2011)

French Words I Use series by Sue Finnie and Daniele Bourdais
(Franklin Watts, 2010)

Index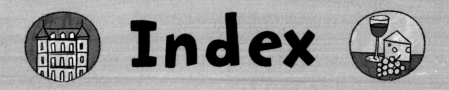